DISCARDED

Math Matters!

Decimals

Look out for these sections to help you learn more about each topic:

Remember...
This provides a summary of the key concept(s) on each two-page entry. Use it to revise what you have learned.

Word check
These are new and important words that help you understand the ideas presented on each two-page entry.

All of the word check entries in this book are shown in the glossary on page 45. The versions in the glossary are sometimes more extensive explanations.

Book link...
Although this book can be used on its own, other titles in the *Math Matters!* set may provide more information on certain topics. This section tells you which other titles to refer to.

Place value
To make it easy for you to see exactly what we are doing, you will find colored columns behind the numbers in all the examples on this and the following pages. This is what the colors mean:

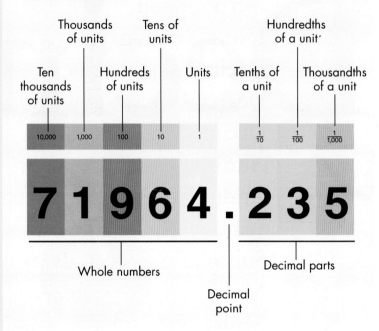

Series concept by *Brian Knapp and Duncan McCrae*
Text contributed by *Brian Knapp and Colin Bass*
Design and production by *Duncan McCrae*
Illustrations of characters by *Nicolas Debon*
Digital illustrations by *David Woodroffe*
Other illustrations by *Peter Bull Art Studio*
Editing by *Lorna Gilbert and Barbara Carragher*
Layout by *Duncan McCrae and Mark Palmer*
Reprographics by *Global Colour*
Printed and bound by *LEGO SpA*

First Published in the United States in 1999 by Grolier Educational, Sherman Turnpike, Danbury, CT 06816

Copyright © 1999
Atlantic Europe Publishing Company Limited

Library of Congress Cataloging-in-Publication Data
Math Matters!
    p. cm.
    Includes indexes.
    Contents: v.1.Numbers — v.2.Adding — v.3.Subtracting — v.4.Multiplying — v.5.Dividing — v.6.Decimals — v.7.Fractions – v.8.Shape — v.9.Size — v.10.Tables and Charts — v.11.Grids and Graphs — v.12.Chance and Average — v.13.Mental Arithmetic
ISBN 0–7172–9294–0 (set: alk. paper). — ISBN 0–7172–9295–9 (v.1: alk. paper). — ISBN 0–7172–9296–7 (v.2: alk. paper). — ISBN 0–7172–9297–5 (v.3: alk. paper). — ISBN 0–7172–9298–3 (v.4: alk. paper). — ISBN 0–7172–9299–1 (v.5: alk. paper). — ISBN 0–7172–9300–9 (v.6: alk. paper). — ISBN 0–7172–9301–7 (v.7: alk. paper). — ISBN 0–7172–9302–5 (v.8: alk. paper). — ISBN 0–7172–9303–3 (v.9: alk. paper). — ISBN 0–7172–9304–1 (v.10: alk. paper). — ISBN 0–7172–9305–X (v.11: alk. paper). — ISBN 0–7172–9306–8 (v.12: alk. paper). — ISBN 0–7172–9307–6 (v.13: alk. paper).

    1. Mathematics — Juvenile literature. [1. Mathematics.]
I. Grolier Educational Corporation.
QA40.5.M38   1998
510 — dc21   98–7404
                                                    CIP
                                                    AC

Contents

4 Introduction

6 Using a decimal point

8 Decimals as shapes

10 Decimals in money

12 Decimals in science

14 Adding with decimals

16 Adding decimals of different lengths

18 Subtracting decimals by exchanging

20 Subtracting decimals by regrouping

22 Multiplying a decimal by a whole number

24 Multiplying with decimals

26 More on multiplying with decimals

28 Checking the decimal point

30 Dividing a decimal by a whole number

32 Changing fractions into decimals

34 Recurring decimals

36 Rounding decimals

38 Changing decimals into fractions

40 Dividing a decimal by a decimal

42 Comparing decimals

44 What symbols mean

45 Glossary

46 Set index

Introduction

37.9

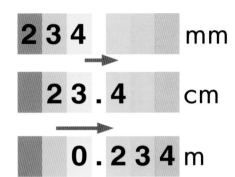

234 mm
→
23.4 cm
→
0.234 m

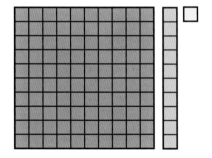

Decimal. This strange word comes from the Latin word *decima*, which means a tenth. A decimal system is therefore a set of rules that are based on tenths. This can apply to money (most modern money systems, or currencies, are based on 10's) or to measurement, as in the metric system.

But when people talk about decimals, they most often mean a number with a period or point in it. There are whole numbers to the left of the period and parts of whole numbers to the right of the period.

```
   0.56
 + 1.96
 ------
   2.52
```

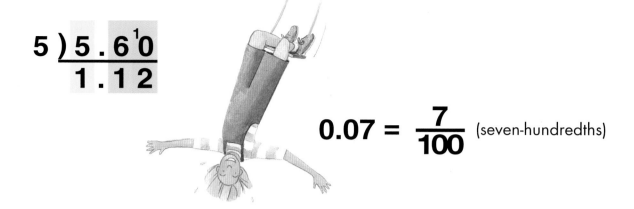

$$5 \overline{) 5.6{}^{1}0}$$
$$1.12$$

$$0.07 = \frac{7}{100} \quad \text{(seven-hundredths)}$$

In fact, we meet this form of decimal all the time, because things rarely come in exact quantities. Few of the items we buy, for example, are bought in whole numbers.

But the really important thing to remember about working with decimals is that it means doing things in tens, whether it is money or measurement, or whether the numbers are bigger or smaller than one. And because ten is such an easy number to work with, you will find that decimals are surprisingly easy whatever form they take.

3.141592654...

$$\frac{3}{4} = 0.75$$

0.397
is bigger than
0.395

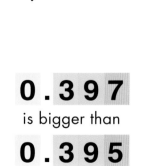

Using a decimal point

Numbers with decimal parts must be written down very carefully. Otherwise you will not be able to see how big these numbers really are. The diagram below shows you how to write out a decimal number correctly. Notice that we have used colored columns to make it easier to see the value of each number. An explanation of these columns is on page 2.

We separate the whole numbers from the parts by using a mathematical period, called a <u>decimal point</u>. It is shown by the "." symbol.

The number on the right is 1.23; that is, one whole unit, two tenths of a unit, and three hundredths of a unit. It is said as "One point two three."

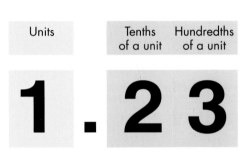

Units		Tenths of a unit	Hundredths of a unit

1.23

← Whole numbers | Decimal point | Decimal parts →

This is the same number but with the columns taken away. The decimal point still marks the end of the whole numbers. Everything to the left of the decimal point is in whole numbers; everything to the right of it consists of parts of whole numbers.

1.23

Take a larger number like 325.23.

Hundreds	Tens	Units		Tenths	Hundredths
3	**2**	**5**	**.**	**2**	**3**

Whole numbers

Parts of whole numbers

← The further a number is to the left, the larger its value.

→ The further the number is to the right, the smaller its value.

We can see how it is made up of hundreds, tens, and units, and then (to the <u>right</u> of the decimal point) tenths and hundredths of units.

	Hundreds	Tens	Units	Point	Tenths	Hundredths	
+	**3**	**0**	**0**				Three hundreds
+		**2**	**0**				Two tens
+			**5**				Five units
+			**0**	**.**	**2**		Two tenths
+			**0**	**.**	**0**	**3**	Three hundredths
=	**3**	**2**	**5**	**.**	**2**	**3**	

This is the number without the colored columns. It is three hundred and twenty five point two three.

3 2 5 . 2 3

Remember... The decimal point tells us which are whole units and which are parts of units.

Word check

Decimal point: A dot written after the units when a number contains parts of a unit as well as whole numbers.

Decimals as shapes

If you are not sure what a decimal number is, then one way to understand it is to write out the problem in shapes, such as those shown below.

    You might want to make your own shapes to work out other problems.

Let's begin with a whole number, in this case **237**. It is made up of hundreds, tens, and units.

Hundreds of units	Tens of units	Units
2	**3**	**7**

We could represent this number by shapes, such as these:

Two hundred
Hundreds

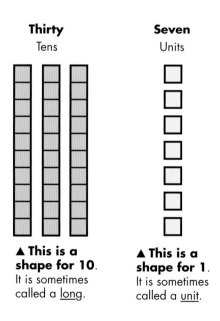

▲ **This is a shape for 100.**
It is sometimes called a <u>flat</u>.

Thirty
Tens

▲ **This is a shape for 10.**
It is sometimes called a <u>long</u>.

Seven
Units

▲ **This is a shape for 1.**
It is sometimes called a <u>unit</u>.

Each shape is ten times bigger than its neighbor to the right.

You can also use this system to represent a number containing a decimal point. Here we make the unit shape bigger to see that it, in turn, contains smaller shapes.

A unit is made up of ten tenths or a hundred hundredths. In this case a <u>long</u> then represents a tenth, and a unit represents a hundredth. See below how it is used to show 2.45.

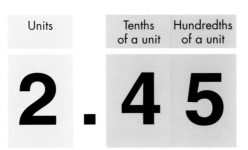

Units	Tenths of a unit	Hundredths of a unit
2 .	**4**	**5**

Two	**Point**	**Four**	**Five**
Units		Tenths	Hundredths

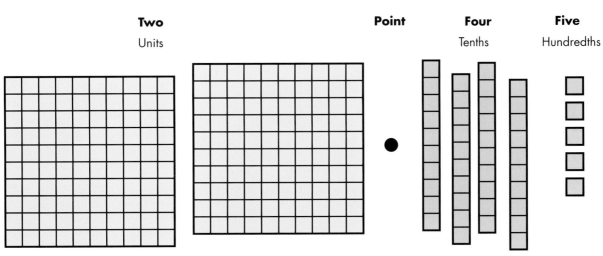

Remember... Whatever size your number, the neighboring numbers are always ten times smaller on the right, and they are less than one if they are to the right of the decimal point.

Word check
Flat: A large square representing 100.
Long: A long shape representing 10.
Unit: A small square shape representing 1.

Decimals in money

All around the world people have realized that it is easier to use a money system in which numbers are multiples of ten.

Almost every currency in the world uses the decimal system to count in tens. The names for whole units and parts of a unit may be different, but they are all decimal currencies.

How we write a decimal currency depends on the unit we are using. For example, if we are using dollars, 23 cents is written down as $0.23, because 23 cents is less than a dollar. But if we are using cents, then 23 cents is expressed in whole numbers because the unit is the cent.

The same is true for other currencies, as you can see.

Dollars and cents

The dollar is the most widely used unit in the world. But a dollar is a large unit, and so there are also coins with a value of part of a dollar, for example, 10 cents and 1 cent. There are 100 cents in a dollar.

The dollar is a decimal currency because cents, tens of cents, and dollars (hundreds of cents) are all multiples of ten.

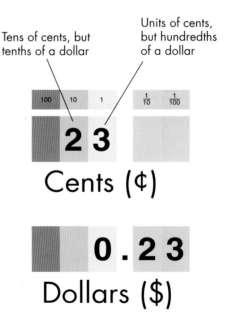

Tens of cents, but tenths of a dollar

Units of cents, but hundredths of a dollar

| 100 | 10 | 1 | | $\frac{1}{10}$ | $\frac{1}{100}$ |

2 3
Cents (¢)

0.2 3
Dollars ($)

23 cents is two 10-cent coins and three 1-cent coins.

Pounds and pence

The pound is the unit of currency of the United Kingdom. There are coins with a value of part of a pound, for example, 10 pence and 1 pence. A pound is made up of 100 pence.

The pound is a decimal currency because there are pence, tens of pence, and hundreds of pence.

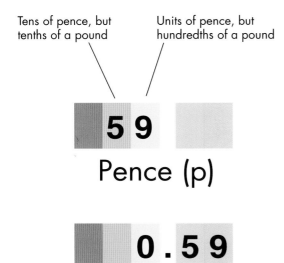

Tens of pence, but tenths of a pound

Units of pence, but hundredths of a pound

5 9

Pence (p)

0 . 5 9

Pounds (£)

59 pence is five 10-pence coins and nine 1-pence coins.

Rupees and paisa

The rupee is the unit of currency of India. There are also coins with a value of part of a rupee, for example, 10 paisa and 1 paisa. A rupee consists of 100 paisa.

Because there are paisa, tens of paisa, and rupees (hundreds of paisa), the rupee is also a decimal currency.

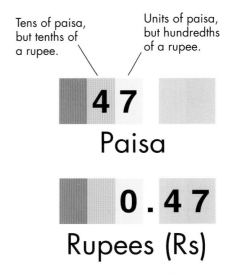

Tens of paisa, but tenths of a rupee.

Units of paisa, but hundredths of a rupee.

4 7

Paisa

0 . 4 7

Rupees (Rs)

47 paisa is four 10-paisa coins and seven 1-paisa coins.

Remember... The world works in decimal currencies, meaning that they are organized in multiples of ten.

Word check
Decimal number: A number that contains parts of units as well as whole units. The decimal point is used to separate the units from the parts of a unit.

Decimals in science

Science works with the metric system of meters, centimeters, and millimeters.

It is fairly simple to change between measurements in millimeters, centimeters, and meters by moving the numbers around the decimal point. These examples show how to do it.

In this example the height of a liquid in a flask was measured using a scale in millimeters. We found it was exactly 234 mm high.

In this case all of the numbers would be to the left of the decimal point, and so the decimal point is not used at all.

100	10	1	$\frac{1}{10}$	$\frac{1}{100}$	$\frac{1}{1,000}$

2 3 4   mm

We could also have recorded the height in centimeters (centimeters are ten times as big as millimeters).

To change our measurement from millimeters to centimeters, we need to divide by 10: So, 234 ÷ 10 = 23.4 cm.

Notice that when we divide by 10, we move the numbers one place to the right.

2 3 . 4   cm

→

Move the numbers
1 place right.

We could also have recorded the height in meters (meters are **100** times as big as centimeters).

To change our measurement from centimeters to meters, we need to divide by 100: 23.4 ÷ 100 = 0.234 m

Notice that when we divide by 100, we move the numbers two places to the right.

0 . 2 3 4 m

→

Move the numbers
2 places right.

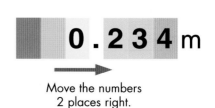

Here is another example for you to look at. In this case we read in meters first, then change to centimeters, and finally millimeters.

The height of the liquid in another flask has been read as 0.379 m.

There are 100 cm in a meter. If we wanted to express the number as centimeters, we would multiply it by 100:

0.379 × 100 = 37.9 cm

Notice that when we multiply by 100, we move the numbers two places to the left.

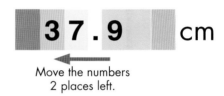

Move the numbers 2 places left.

We could also express the height in millimeters. There are 10 millimeters in a centimeter. To change to millimeters, we multiply by 10, moving the numbers one place to the left:

37.9 × 10 = 379 mm

3 7 9 mm

Move the numbers 1 place left.

Remember… When we <u>divide</u> a number by 10, we move the numbers one place to the <u>right</u>. This is the same as moving the decimal point one place to the <u>left</u>.

When we <u>multiply</u> a number by 10, we move the numbers one place to the <u>left</u>. This is the same as moving the decimal point one place to the <u>right</u>.

Word check

Decimal place: The digits used for parts of a unit, such as tenths and hundredths. For example, if a number is given to "2 decimal places," it means that there are digits in the tenths and hundredths columns.

Adding with decimals

To add with decimals, you first have to line up each number at the decimal point.

Once the decimal points have been lined up, adding with decimals becomes the same as ordinary addition.

For example, **345.23 + 467.39 = ?**

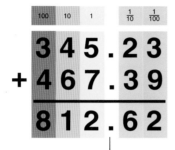

100	10	1	$\frac{1}{10}$	$\frac{1}{100}$

$$
\begin{array}{r}
3\ 4\ 5\ .\ 2\ 3 \\
+\ 4\ 6\ 7\ .\ 3\ 9 \\
\hline
8\ 1\ 2\ .\ 6\ 2
\end{array}
$$

Put the decimal point in the answer in line with the other decimal points.

Decimal stretch

Jilly was working on a science project. She had discovered that a rubber band stretched **0.56** cm when she hung a **100** g weight from it, and **1.96** cm when she hung a **350** g weight from it.

Jilly then needed to add together the two measurements she had made to find out how far the rubber band would stretch if she hung a **450** g weight from it. For this she needed to add two decimal numbers, as you can see here.

The answer was 2.52.

A zero (0) is written here to make it absolutely clear that the number is less than 1.

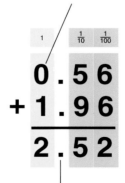

1	$\frac{1}{10}$	$\frac{1}{100}$

$$
\begin{array}{r}
0\ .\ 5\ 6 \\
+\ 1\ .\ 9\ 6 \\
\hline
2\ .\ 5\ 2
\end{array}
$$

The numbers are lined up and then added together in the normal way.

Book link... This is an example of proportion. The stretching is proportional to the weight. See the book *Fractions* in the *Math Matters!* set.

Making decimals whole numbers while you add

If you are still unsure about adding decimal numbers, you can turn them into whole numbers simply by making the decimal parts the same length, then dropping the decimal point. Add the whole numbers together, and then put the decimal point back into the answer. Here is an example to show how it is done.

James wanted to measure the length of two pieces of wood he was working on. The first length of wood measured 3.56 m, and the second length measured 4.76 m. Notice the decimal point is two numbers from the right in each case.

Step 1: Since he did not feel sure about decimals yet, he decided to turn his decimals into whole numbers while he added.

Step 2: He lined up both numbers so the decimal points were above one another. Then he removed the decimal point.

In this way 3.56 became 356, and 4.76 became 476. He added 356 + 476 together. The total was 832.

Step 3: Finally, he had to convert his number back to a decimal number, so he placed the decimal point two numbers from the right in his answer, so that 832 became 8.32 m.

Remember... To add with decimals, either add normally, making sure you line up the numbers around the decimal point, or convert to whole numbers, add them together, and then convert back.

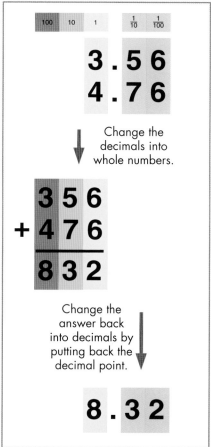

| 100 | 10 | 1 | $\frac{1}{10}$ | $\frac{1}{100}$ |

3 . 5 6
4 . 7 6

Change the decimals into whole numbers.

$$\begin{array}{r} 356 \\ + 476 \\ \hline 832 \end{array}$$

Change the answer back into decimals by putting back the decimal point.

8 . 3 2

Adding decimals of different lengths

There is no fixed length for a decimal number. It may have one number to the right of the decimal point, two, three, or even more.

If you find that you have numbers of a different length to the right of the decimal point to add together, you need to follow this rule.

Line up the two numbers using the decimal point.

100	10	1		$\frac{1}{10}$	$\frac{1}{100}$
2	7	6 .		3	5
	5	6 .		1	

Suppose we have two unequal numbers such as 276.35 and 56.1. When we line them up using the decimal point, we notice something strange – they are not the same length!

But the numbers can still be added together. We simply need to put a 0 in the space as shown in the example:

```
2 7 6 . 3 5
  5 6 . 1 0
```

Fill in a 0 here.

Then we can do the adding.

```
  2 7 6 . 3 5
+   5 6 . 1 0
  ─────────────
  3 3 2 . 4 5
```

Suppose we have a whole number such as **357** and a decimal number such as **39.37**. The whole number does not appear to be a decimal number. But we can convert it into a decimal number simply by adding a decimal point and a **0** after the whole number.

3 5 7
3 9 . 3 7

Place a decimal point here.

Fill in a 0 here for every decimal place of the other number.

Notice that in this case we needed to add two **0**'s to make both numbers the same length as well as adding a decimal point.

3 5 7 . 0 0
3 9 . 3 7

Then we can do the adding.

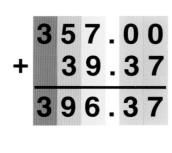

$$
\begin{array}{r}
357.00 \\
+\ \ 39.37 \\
\hline
396.37
\end{array}
$$

Remember... To add whole numbers and decimals, turn the whole number into a decimal by adding a decimal point and as many **0**'s as neccessary.

Subtracting decimals by exchanging

To subtract two numbers, first put the number you are subtracting below the one you are subtracting from, making sure the decimal points line up.

Then begin subtracting starting from the right.

The method of subtracting shown on these two pages is known as the "exchanging" method.

Step 1: In this example we are subtracting the decimal 26.39 from the decimal 34.23. First line up the two numbers using the decimal points.

$$34.23 - 26.39 = ?$$

Both numbers line up around the decimal point.

10	1		$\frac{1}{10}$	$\frac{1}{100}$
3	4	.	2	3
2	6	.	3	9

Step 2: Start subtracting on the right (in this case the hundredths column). Subtract the lower number from the upper number. Because 3 − 9 won't work, exchange one from the tenths column on the left, and balance this out by adding 1 to the lower number of the tenths column as shown.

Now the subtraction is 13 − 9 = 4. Write down 4 in the hundredths column of the answer line.

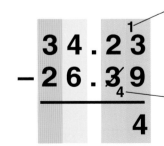

Exchange 1 from the tenths column, making a total of 13 hundredths.

Balance this out by adding 1 to the lower number of the tenths column.

Step 3: Moving to the next column on the left (the tenths column), we find that 2 − 4 won't work. Again, we need to exchange, but this time it is between the units and the tenths columns as shown. Now we are left with 12 − 4 = 8. Write down 8 in the tenths column.

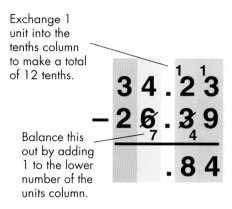

Exchange 1 unit into the tenths column to make a total of 12 tenths.

Balance this out by adding 1 to the lower number of the units column.

Step 4: Moving to the units column, we find that 4 − 7 won't work. Exchange between the tens and units columns as shown.

We now have 14 − 7 = 7. Write down 7 in the units column.

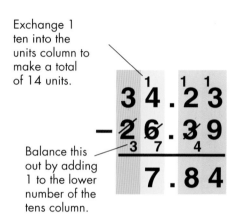

Exchange 1 ten into the units column to make a total of 14 units.

Balance this out by adding 1 to the lower number of the tens column.

Step 5: Moving to the tens column, we now have: 3 − 3 = 0. When a zero (0) is the first number, we normally leave it out, and so in this case we are left with an answer of **7.84**.

The subtraction shown on these two pages is known as the "exchanging" method.

Remember... Subtracting with decimals is no different from subtracting with whole numbers. You just have to remember to line up the numbers around the decimal points.

Word check
Exchanging: In subtracting this is the method of taking 1 from the column to the left to use it as 10 at the top of your working column, and adding 1 at the bottom of the left column.

Note... You can subtract by the exchanging method shown on this page or by regrouping, as shown on page 20.

Book link... Find out more about exchanging and regrouping in the book *Subtracting* in the *Math Matters!* set.

Subtracting decimals by regrouping

You may prefer to subtract using the "regrouping" method, which is an alternative to the "exchanging" method shown on pages 18 and 19.

In this case too you will still need to line up the numbers around the decimal points first. But the subtracting uses the following steps.

Step 1: Line up the two numbers using the decimal points. In this case we are subtracting 1.72 from 2.5.

If the numbers have an unequal number of decimals, add extra zeros to fill the columns. In this case a zero (0) has been added to the 2.5 to make it 2.50.

Both numbers line up around the decimal point.

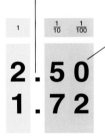

Fill in a 0 here in the hundredths column.

Step 2: Start subtracting on the right (the hundredths column). Take the lower number from the upper. Because 0 − 2 won't work, regroup one tenth as ten hundredths, reducing the tenths from 5 to 4 and increasing the hundredths by 10.

Now the subtraction is 10 − 2 = 8. Write down 8 in the answer line.

Regroup 1 tenth from the top of the tenths column to add 10 hundredths at the top of the hundredths column. Cross out the 0, and write a 10.

This leaves 4 tenths in the tenths column. Cross out the 5, and write a 4.

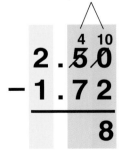

Step 3: Now move to the next column on the left; the tenths column. Because we cannot take 7 from 4, we need to regroup 1 unit as 10 tenths, reduce the units to 1, and increase the tenths to 14.

Now we are left with the subtraction: 14 − 7 = 7. Write down 7 in the tenths column of the answer line.

Regroup one of the 2 units as 10 tenths, and reduce it to 1. Make the top of the tenths column 14 tenths.

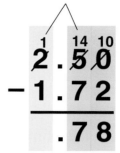

Step 4: Moving left to the units column, 1 − 1 = 0. When a zero (0) is the first number, we normally leave it out, but here we write down the 0 to make it clear that this decimal answer is less than 1. The answer to this subtraction is 0.78.

The subtraction shown on these two pages is known as "regrouping" method.

Remember... You can subtract by regrouping or by exchanging, as shown on page 18.

Word check

Regrouping: In subtracting this is the method of moving 1 from the top of the column to the left to use it as 10 at the top of your working column.

Book link... Find out more about exchanging and regrouping in the book *Subtracting* in the *Math Matters!* set.

Multiplying a decimal by a whole number

If you have to multiply a decimal by
a whole number, you can use this
simple technique.

Here we want to multiply **6.5 × 7 = ?**

We are multiplying a decimal by a
whole number. We can do this in a
few steps:

100	10	1	$\frac{1}{10}$

Step 1: Count and remember how
many places of decimals you have.
In this case it is **1** place.

The decimal number 6.5
has been moved one
place to the left to make
the whole number 65.

Step 2: Convert the decimal number
to a whole number.

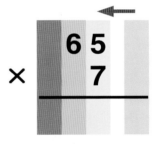

Step 3: Multiply as you would for two
whole numbers. That is: 7 × 65 = 455.

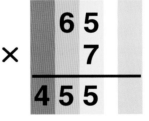

Step 4: Now change the answer from a
whole number back into a decimal
number by moving the number to the
right the same number of places as in the
original decimal number.

   In this case the number goes **1** place
to the right. Notice the difference this
makes to the value of the answer. It
divides it by **10** from **455** to **45.5**.

Move the whole number
455 one place to the right,
and insert the decimal
point to turn it back to the
decimal number 45.5.

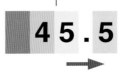

Why does it work?

This method works because you really multiplied the decimal number by 10 when you moved the number one place to the left. Then you divided the answer by 10 to make it correct again when you moved the number back.

In step one on the opposite page we multiplied 6.5 by 10 to make the whole number 65.

$$6.5 \times 10 = 65$$

In step four on the opposite page we divided 455 by 10 to make the decimal 45.5 and give the answer to the original calculation.

$$455 \div 10 = 45.5$$

More practice

If we wanted to multiply 7 meters × 6.15 meters, you would have needed to move the number two places to the left to produce a whole number.

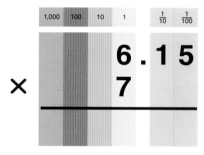

The number 6.15 is moved two places to the left.

The multiplication would become 7 × 615 = 4,305.

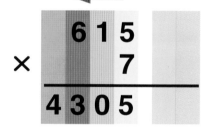

A decimal point would need to be put into the answer two places from the right-hand end. That makes it 43.05. This is because 6.15 was multiplied by 100 when the number was moved, and 4,305 was divided by 100 when the number was moved back.

The number is moved two places to the right.

Remember... To replace the decimal point correctly when multiplying.

Word check

Decimal place: The digits used for parts of a unit, such as tenths and hundredths. For example, if a number is given to "2 decimal places," it means that there are digits in the tenths and hundredths columns.

Multiplying with decimals

Two decimal numbers can be multiplied together by first turning both of them into whole numbers.

Measuring the weed killer

Sean's and Kelly's dad wanted to buy some weed killer for the lawn on his way home from work. Unfortunately, he had forgotten to measure the lawn. He telephoned to ask the children to measure it for him. The lawn was shaped like a rectangle. Dad asked the children to measure the length and the width of the lawn in meters, and then multiply the two figures together to find out the total area of the lawn.

Sean measured the lawn very carefully. It was 7.1 m long and 6.2 m wide.

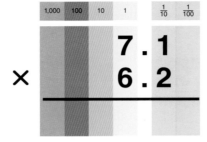

To multiply these numbers, the children first multiplied each number by 10. By doing this, they converted the decimal numbers to whole numbers.

Now they could multiply as normal. The answer was 4,402.

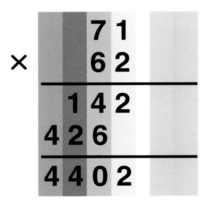

However, because they had multiplied each number by 10, and 10 × 10 = 100, the final answer was 100 times too big! So they had to <u>divide</u> by 100, which meant moving the number two places to the right. This made the correct answer 44.02.

Sean's and Kelly's dad was very pleased when they told him their answer.

When he arrived at the shop, he discovered that the weed killer was sold in packs containing enough to treat either 30 square meters or 50 square meters. Dad could therefore confidently buy the 50-square-meter pack because he now knew that the 30-square-meter pack would be too small.

30 < 44 < 50

Word check
<: The symbol for less than.

Remember… Multiplying your way out of trouble is fine. But you do have to put the decimal point back at the end!

Book link… Find out more about rectangles in *Shape*. Find out more about areas in *Size*, and find out more about multiplying big numbers in *Multiplying* in the *Math Matters!* set.

More on multiplying with decimals

Here is an extension of the rule for remembering where to put the decimal point. It applies to all numbers.

To multiply two decimal numbers

Step 1: For the calculation 2.25 multiplied by 1.23, move the number to the left-hand end of both decimal numbers, turning them into whole numbers.

Step 2: Count and remember how many places you moved them. In both cases the numbers have been moved two places to the left, so the total number of places moved is 4.

2.25 × 1.23 = ?

In both cases the decimal point is moved two places to the right to make the decimal numbers into whole numbers. These moves add up to total of 4 decimal places.

2.25 ⇨ 225

1.23 ⇨ 123

Step 3: Multiply the whole numbers together in the normal way.

Book link... Find out more on multiplication in the book *Multiplying* in the *Math Matters!* set.

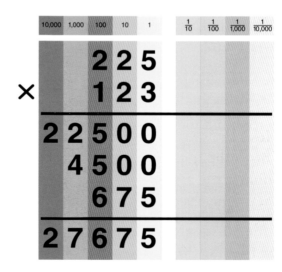

Step 4: Finally, change the answer from a whole number back into a decimal number by moving the number back from the left-hand end the total number of places counted in step 2.

2.7675

More about the lawn

Let's try using this rule on Sean's and Kelly's lawn (see page 25). Suppose Kelly measured it as 7.1 m × 6.15 m. Notice that the two measurements do not have the same number of decimal places in them.

Change 7.1 into 71 and remember that the number has been moved 1 place.

Change 6.15 into 615 and remember that the number has been moved 2 places. This makes 3 places altogether.

Multiply 71 × 615 = 43,665

Move the number to the right 3 places. This is the same as placing a decimal point in the answer 3 decimal places back from the right-hand end. In this way Sean and Kelly find out that the lawn area measures 43.665 m².

Remember... You put the decimal point in the answer as many places from the right as the total decimal places in the numbers you multiplied.

$$6.15 \times 7.1 = ?$$

In this case the decimal point is moved one place to the right to change the decimal number 7.1 into the whole number 71.

For the decimal number 6.15 the decimal point is moved two places to the right to produce the whole number 615.

The moves for these two decimal numbers add up to total of 3 decimal places.

7.1 ⇨ 71

6.15 ⇨ 615

```
        6 1 5
×         7 1
─────────────
        6 1 5
    4 3 0 5 0
─────────────
    4 3 6 6 5
```

4 3 . 6 6 5

Word check
m²: Meters squared.

Checking the decimal point

It is a good idea to check your math work by a different method whenever you can.

We all make mistakes. It pays to find your own before anyone else does! It is especially useful when working with decimals to make sure that you have the decimal point in the right place.

Here is a quick method of checking that you have the right answer when multiplying.

The method

Step 1: Write down the numbers you want to multiply together using only the number furthest to the left. Write 0's in place of the others, and you have a simpler number to work with.

Step 2: Multiply these two simpler numbers in your head, taking care about the total number of 0's in your answer.

This should give you the approximate size of answer to the multiplication you are checking.

For example, suppose we want to multiply 52.34 by 14 using the method above.

$$52.34 \times 14 = ?$$

Step 1: 52.34 becomes 50 because the number furthest to the left is in the tens column.

14 becomes 10 because the left-hand number is in the tens column.

$$52.34 \Rightarrow 50$$
$$14 \Rightarrow 10$$

Step 2: $50 \times 10 = 500$

So when we multiply 52.34 by 14, we know our answer is around 500.

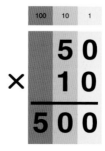

100	10	1
	5	0
×	1	0
5	0	0

This is the rough answer worked out using long multiplication.

When we work the sum out using long multiplication, the answer is exactly 732.76. But you can see that the rough check at least made sure that we knew the answer was in the hundreds rather than in the tens, thousands, and so on. And this check took only a few seconds.

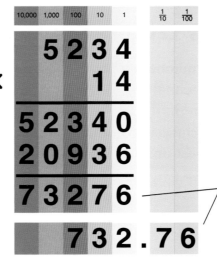

This is the exact answer worked out using long multiplication of the whole numbers and then replacing the decimal point as shown on page 26.

Book link... Find out more on multiplication in the book *Multiplying* in the *Math Matters!* set.

Another example, checking huge numbers also uses "rounding." For the calculation 5,678 × 87.65.

5,678 × 87.65 = ?

Step 1: Round up 5,678 to 6,000 and 87.65 to 90.

5,678 ⇨ 6,000
87.65 ⇨ 90

Now the problem is 6,000 × 90.

6,000 × 90

Split up the long numbers to make them shorter and therefore easier to multiply.
  You can now multiply the simple numbers in your head in any order you wish to make the approximate answer 540,000.

= 6 × 9 × 1,000 × 10
= 54 × 10,000
= 540,000

The correct answer is 497,676.7, and as you can see, 540,000 is near enough to make us sure that we are getting the decimal point in the right place.

Remember... Rough working out only takes a few seconds, and these few seconds are well spent if we can be sure that the decimal point is in the right place.

Word check
Rounding: Making a number simpler.

Book link... Find out more about rounding off numbers in the book *Grids and Graphs* in the *Math Matters!* set and on page 36 of this book.
  Find easy ways of working out numbers in your head in the book *Mental Arithmetic* in the *Math Matters!* set.

Dividing a decimal by a whole number

When dividing a whole number into a decimal, just keep the decimal points lined up, and the decimal point in the answer will automatically be in the correct position.

You can use either short or long division.

Pizza sharing

José bought a pizza for $5.60 for himself and four friends. They divided it equally among the five of them and ate it. At the end of the meal the four friends wanted to pay José what they owed him.

The calculation was

$$5.60 \div 5 = ?$$

They did this by short division as follows:

Step 1: Divide 5 into the first digit. The answer is 1, remainder 0. Put in a decimal point.

$$5 \overline{)\ 5.6\ 0}$$
$$1.\ ?\ ?$$

Step 2: Divide 5 into the second digit, 6. The answer is 1 remainder 1. Carry the remainder right to make 10.

$$5 \overline{)\ 5.6\ {}^{1}0}$$
$$1.1\ ?$$

Step 3: Divide 5 into the third number, 10. The answer is 2, remainder 0.

$$5 \overline{)\ 5.6\ {}^{1}0}$$
$$1.12$$

So each friend had to pay José $1.12.

Ben works it out

Ben wanted to compare accurately the thickness of a cassette box and a CD box. He stacked a sample of 15 cassettes along a table and measured the total length very carefully. It was 25.45 cm.

It was now easy for Ben to work out accurately how thick one of the cassette cases would be.

This is how Ben worked it out:

Step 1: Divide 15 into the first two digits. The answer is 1 with a remainder of 10. Put in a decimal point. Bring down the next number, making 104.

Step 2: Divide 15 into the remainder (104). The answer is 6 with a remainder of 14. Bring down the next digit, 5, to make 145.

Step 3: Divide 15 into the remainder, 145. The answer is 9 with a remainder of 10.

Steps 4 onward: Divide 15 into the remainder, and so on to get as many decimal places as you want.

The answer was 1.6966 centimeters. Then he repeated the experiment with 15 CD boxes. You might like to find out how thick a CD box is using this method.

Remember... To divide whole numbers into decimals, you can use either short or long division.

```
               1 . 6 9 6 6
      _____
1 5 ) 2 5 . 4 5 0 0
      1 5
      _____
      1 0   4
          9   0
      _____
          1   4 5
          1   3 5
          _____
                1 0 0
                    9 0
                _____
                    1 0  etc.
```

Word check
Digit: The numerals 1, 2, 3, 4, 5, 6, 7, 8, 9, or 0. Several may be used to stand for a larger number. They are called digits to make it clear that they are only part of a complete number. So we might say, "The second digit is 4," meaning the second numeral from the left. Or we might say, "That is a two-digit number," meaning that it has two numerals in it, tens and units.

Changing fractions into decimals

Decimal numbers smaller than one can be expressed as fractions. Similarly, fractions can be expressed as decimals.

Here you can see how to change fractions into decimals.

You need only to divide the numerator (top number) by the denominator (bottom number).

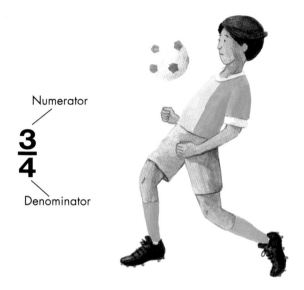

Numerator

$\dfrac{3}{4}$

Denominator

If the numbers are easy, you might be able to do that in your head, and you will soon remember the common ones. For example ¾ (three-quarters) is exactly 0.75.

$$\dfrac{3}{4} = 0.75$$

If you cannot do the division in your head, write it down. You can use short or long division.

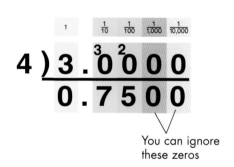

| 1 | $\frac{1}{10}$ | $\frac{1}{100}$ | $\frac{1}{1,000}$ | $\frac{1}{10,000}$ |

$$4\,)\,3.\overset{3}{0}\overset{2}{0}00$$
$$0.7500$$

In many cases, after a few decimal places the division will complete, and there will be no remainder. The fraction ¾ is such an example. By short division ¾ works out to 0.75 exactly. Here is the working:

You can ignore these zeros

Here is another example. If we look at the fraction ¾

$$\frac{9}{4}$$

by short division ¾ works out to 2.25 exactly. We worked it out like this...

$$4\overline{)9.0^{1}0^{2}000}$$
$$2.2500$$

Common conversions

Here are some conversions that are often used in everyday life. Try to remember these.

⅒	(a tenth)	=	0.1
¹⁄₁₀₀	(a hundredth)	=	0.01
¹⁄₁₀₀₀	(a thousandth)	=	0.001
½	(a half)	=	0.5
¼	(a quarter)	=	0.25
¾	(three-quarters)	=	0.75

Sometimes, when we are converting a fraction to a decimal, the decimal number will not be completed but will carry on producing new digits forever. Mathematicians call this a <u>recurring decimal</u>. Find out more about this on page 34.

It's common to see fractions and decimals together, as on this ruler.

This scale is divided into fractional lengths of ½, ¼, etc.

This scale is decimal; 0.1, 0.2, etc.

Remember... Every fraction can be converted into a decimal by dividing the top number by the bottom number.

Word Check

Denominator: The number written on the bottom of a fraction.

Numerator: The number written on the top of a fraction.

Recurring decimals

Sometimes when you try to convert a fraction to a decimal, the calculation cannot be completed even if you carried on forever. Mathematicians call this a "recurring decimal."

One-third (⅓) is a very common fraction. It converts into a recurring decimal. Here is the working, done by long division.

3 divides into 10 3 times with a remainder of 1. Bring down a 0... and 3 divides into 10 3 times with a remainder of 1... And so on forever.

The answer is: 0.3333333333333333 3333333333333333333333333... forever. Mathematicians say this as "point three recurring."

```
          0 . 3 3 3 3 3
    3 ) 1 . 0 0 0 0 0
            9
            1 0
              9
              1 0
                9
                1 0
                  9
                  1 0
                    9
                         etc.
```

Not exactly...

Of course, 0.33 (using just the first two decimal places) is <u>not</u> exactly one-third.

The decimal number 0.33 is exactly the same as the fraction ³³⁄₁₀₀, and that is a little less than a third (⅓), as you can see by multiplying it by 3. So, 3 × 33 = 99.

The total is ⁹⁹⁄₁₀₀, which is a little less than 1.

$$0.33 = \frac{99}{100}$$

0.333 is <u>not</u> exactly one-third either.

The decimal number 0.333 is precisely the same as the fraction ³³³⁄₁₀₀₀, and that is also a little less than a third (⅓), as you can see by multiplying it by 3. So, 3 × 333 = 999.

The total is ⁹⁹⁹⁄₁₀₀₀, which is a little less than 1.

$$0.333 = \frac{999}{1,000}$$

That can go on infinitely too. But if the decimal 0.33333333333333333333333333 goes on forever, it will be <u>exactly</u> one-third.

Here is a story to help you see why that should be the case.

Eating ice cream forever and ever...

Gill has a **1**-kg (or **1,000**-g) tub of ice cream to share among nine children. They are very eager to see that it is shared equally.

She cannot measure exactly ⅑ th of a kilogram, so she measures ¹⁄₁₀ th (**0.1** kg, or **100** g). The children each have a portion, and instead of eating the tenth portion herself, Gill keeps it for "second helpings."

Since this portion is **100** g, she divides it in the same way, keeping one portion back for "third helpings" and giving each child **10** g or **0.01** kg.

Using this system, the children could go on eating smaller and smaller portions of ice cream forever!

If Gill could go on dividing it in the same way until there was absolutely none left, each child would have had exactly ⅑ th of it.

This tells us the very strange result that:

0.1 + **0.01** + **0.001** + **0.0001** + and so on forever...

$$= \frac{1}{9}$$ exactly.

Word Check

Recurring decimal: A decimal that shows new digits however many decimal places are used. There is always a repeating pattern, so although the digits go on forever, we know what they are.

Remember... A recurring decimal never ends.

Rounding decimals

Calculators make division easy. But when you use them to divide, you can get a "stampede" of numbers after the decimal point whether you are dividing whole numbers or decimal numbers. Here is how to avoid a "stampede."

Calculators do not have a brain to tell them what degree of accuracy to work toward. For example, when you divide **639** by **56** (**639 ÷ 56**) using a calculator, you get **11.41071429.**

It is best to keep working with these long numbers until you reach the very end of your calculation. They help your calculator give you the most accurate answer.

But, since you probably only need a short final answer, perhaps with only a tenths digit and a hundredths digit, you have to "chop off" the string of numbers the calculator produces. This is called rounding off.

Rounding up or down

Once you know what degree of accuracy you need, include one extra digit, and throw the rest away. In this example we have a figure showing **7.1421342** on our calculator, and we want only two decimal places (that is, to include tenths and hundreths).

The rule is this: if the extra digit is **0, 1, 2, 3,** or **4,** throw that away, too. But if it is **5, 6, 7, 8, 9,** then increase the last digit by **1,** and <u>then</u> throw the final digit away.

How to use a calculator
Step 1: Enter 639
Step 2: Press division sign (/ or ÷)
Step 3: Enter 56
Step 4: Press equals sign (=)
    (Answer reads 11.41071429)

Below are the numbers you throw away.

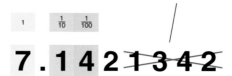

If you want an answer that is accurate to 2 decimal places, look at the third decimal place. Since it is less than 5, we can throw it and all of the extra numbers away.

Take a look at another example: $\dfrac{6}{7} = 0.8571428$

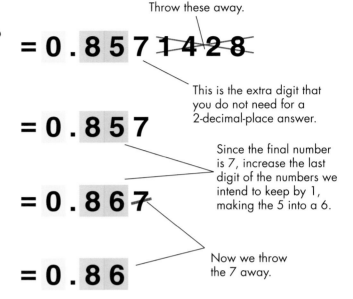

We want an answer that is correct to 2 decimal places, so we throw away the fourth decimal and beyond.

$= 0.8571428$

Throw these away.

This is the extra digit that you do not need for a 2-decimal-place answer.

But we see that the number in the third decimal place is 7.

$= 0.857$

Since the final number is 7, increase the last digit of the numbers we intend to keep by 1, making the 5 into a 6.

So we change the last digit in our answer to 6.

$= 0.867$

$= 0.86$

Now we throw the 7 away.

This diagram shows why we increased the last digit. Clearly, 0.857 is closer to 0.86 than it is to 0.85, which is why it is rounded up to 0.86.

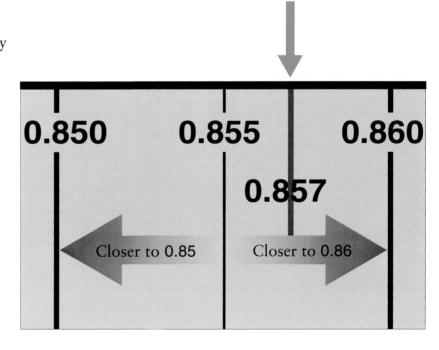

Remember... Decimal numbers are often rounded off. But remember to check the size of the digit just after the last one you want to keep to see if you need to round up or down.

Word check
Rounding: Making a number shorter.

Changing decimals into fractions

Turning decimals into fractions is not always so easy. Here are some hints.

Decimals with an end in sight

These are the simpler ones. To convert a decimal into a fraction, start by multiplying the decimal by **10**, **100**, or whatever number is needed to make the decimal into a whole number. Then simplify the fraction. For example:

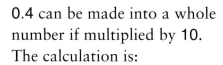

0.4 can be made into a whole number if multiplied by **10**. The calculation is:

$$0.4 = \frac{4}{10} \text{ (four-tenths)}$$

Now simplify the fraction by dividing the top and bottom numbers by **2**.

$$= \overset{4 \div 2}{\frac{2}{5}} \text{ (two-fifths)}$$
$$\underset{10 \div 2}{}$$

Other multiples of tenths are just as easy:

$$0.3 = \frac{3}{10} \text{ (three-tenths)}$$

$$0.07 = \frac{7}{100} \text{ (seven-hundredths)}$$

$$0.25 = \frac{25}{100} \text{ (twenty-five-hundredths)}$$

$$= \overset{25 \div 25}{\frac{1}{4}} \text{ (one-quarter)}$$
$$\underset{100 \div 25}{}$$

Recurring decimals

These are the tricky ones. Mathematicians know how to convert every recurring decimal into an exact fraction, even horrid decimals like 1.696666... which is the fraction $^{509}/_{300}$. Unfortunately, none of these methods is easy.

Pi, the impossible one!

There are some decimals that never end and never recur. However many decimal places are worked out, no repeating pattern can ever be found. There are lots of numbers like this, and a few of them are important.

The most famous is *Pi*. This is the number that you have to multiply the diameter of a circle by to find the circumference.

Throughout history mathematicians have devoted many years to calculating Pi to hundreds of decimal places. This was not because they needed to draw very accurate circles, but because they wanted to write Pi as an exact fraction, and so they hoped that the decimal would eventually recur. In 1882 it was proved that it never, ever would. So people now accept using a close approximate fraction of $^{22}/_{7}$.

3.141592654...

...is approximately equal to $\dfrac{22}{7}$

Book Link... Find out more about Pi in the book *Size* in the *Math Matters!* set.

Word check

Pi: The number of times bigger the circumference of a circle is than the diameter. It is given a special name because it cannot be written down precisely as a fraction or as a decimal. It is approximately $^{22}/_{7}$ or 3.14159265....

Remember... To convert decimals to fractions, it is generally best to remember the conversions because there are not very many.

Dividing a decimal by a decimal

It is not difficult to divide a decimal by a decimal. You simply need to make the number you are dividing by into a whole number first.

Enough for all?

Sun's class was doing a science experiment by boiling salty water to find its temperature. His teacher mixed up 1.5 liters of salty water.

Brian was given a scoop holding 85 milliliters to make up to a 1-liter solution of salty water.

Claudia had to use two scoops of salty water before doing the same, Toto had to use three scoops, Elizabeth had to use four scoops, and Sun had to use five scoops.

Sun was worried that there would not be enough salty water left when it was his turn. He worked out that at least 15 scoops would be needed. He added up his friends' scoops like this: 1 + 2 + 3 + 4 + 5 = 15. To work out whether there will be enough salty water left, he needed to divide 1.5 liters by 85 milliliters. Since there are 1,000 milliliters in a liter, Sun worked out that 85 milliliters was equal to 0.085 liters.

85 milliliters = 0.085 liter

The problem that Sun needed to solve was therefore 1.5 divided by 0.085.

$$1.5 \div 0.085 = ?$$

Multiplying to remove the decimal point

One way around this difficult-looking problem is to turn the decimals into whole numbers by multiplying everything by 1,000. In this way 0.085 becomes 85, and 1.5 becomes 1,500. The division itself hasn't changed because all the numbers were multiplied by the same amount to express them as milliliters.

Now we can use long division. The answer is that there would be 17.6 scoops available.

Clearly this is more than the 15 needed. Sun need not have worried that there would not be enough for him!

Also...

In Sun's calculation the decimal point disappeared from the number he divided by (the divisor) as well as the number he divided into (the dividend). This does not always happen. The important thing is to remember to make the divisor into a whole number before you divide.

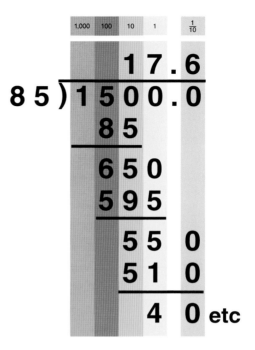

1,000	100	10	1	$\frac{1}{10}$

```
                1 7 . 6
      8 5 ) 1 5 0 0 . 0
              8 5
              6 5 0
              5 9 5
                5 5   0
                5 1   0
                  4   0  etc
```

Book link... For more about long division see the book *Dividing* in the *Math Matters!* set.

Remember... To divide decimal numbers easily, you need to multiply both divisor and dividend by the same number of 10's until the divisor is a whole number.

Word check
Dividend: The number you wish to divide into.
Divisor: The number you divide with.
Quotient: The answer when you divide a dividend by a divisor.

Comparing decimals

It's handy to be able to compare decimal numbers quickly and easily. Here's how.

Units	Tenths of a unit	Hundredths of a unit

Everybody knows that **207** is bigger than **34**. We know this because **207** has a **2** in the hundreds column, while **34** has nothing in the hundreds column. This is true even though **34** has three tens, and **207** doesn't have any.

0.11

This number contains tenths.

It works the same way with decimals. A decimal with something in the tenths column must be bigger than another decimal with **0** in the tenths column.

is bigger than

0.09

This number contains only hundredths, there are no tenths.

Comparing significant figures

If the digits in the first decimal place are different, the one with the bigger digit is the bigger number. So, for example, 0.8239 is bigger than 0.74589, as shown on the right.

0.8239
is bigger than
0.74589
or **0.8239 > 0.74589**

If the first digits are the same, we compare the second digits in the same way.

0.568
is bigger than
0.559
or **0.568 > 0.559**

If the first and second digits are the same, the one with the bigger third digit is the bigger number.

0.397
is bigger than
0.395
or **0.397 > 0.395**

And so on.

Check your measurements

When the decimals represent measurements, we need to be sure that the measurements can be compared (for example, all in meters, not some in meters and others in centimeters).

Here are some lengths arranged in decreasing size. They are all in meters for easy comparison. Any other unit for measuring length could also have been used, as long as it was used for all the examples.

	Meters
Height of this page	0.254
Width of this page	0.195
Height of a postage stamp	0.023
Width of a postage stamp	0.019
Thickness of this book's cover	0.003
Thickness of this paper	0.00012
Thickness of gold leaf	0.00004
Thickness of protective film	0.00002

Remember... To compare the size of decimals, line up the decimal points and compare the digits in each number, starting from the left. If they are equal, move to the next number on the right. If these digits are not the same, whichever is the bigger belongs to the bigger number.

Word check

>: The symbol for more than.

Significant figures: The numbers (reading from the left) that you need for your purpose. This is a way of describing how precise the number is. It is not affected by the position of the decimal point, which has more to do with the units being used.

What symbols mean

Here is a list of the common math symbols together with an example of how they are used. You will find this list in each of the *Math Matters!* books, so that you can turn to any book if you want to look up the meaning of a symbol.

— Between two numbers this symbol means "subtract" or "minus." In front of one number it means the number is negative. In Latin *minus* means "less."

✚ The symbol for adding. We say it "plus." In Latin *plus* means "more."

✖ The symbol for multiplying. We say it "multiplied by" or "times."

═ The symbol for equals. We say it "equals" or "makes." It comes from a Latin word meaning "level" because weighing scales are level when the amounts on each side are equal.

$$(8 + 9 - 3) \times \frac{2}{5} = 5.6$$

( ) Parentheses. You do everything inside the parentheses first. Parentheses always occur in pairs.

—, /, and **÷** Three symbols for dividing. We say it "divided by." A pair of numbers above and below a / or — make a fraction, so ⅖ or $\frac{2}{5}$ is the fraction two-fifths.

■ This is a decimal point. It is a dot written after the units when a number contains parts of a unit as well as whole numbers. This is the decimal number five point six or five and six-tenths.

Glossary

Other symbols used in this book

< : The symbol for less than.

> : The symbol for more than.

m^2: Meters squared. A unit of area the size of a square measuring 1 meter each way.

Terms commonly used in this book.

Decimal number: A number that contains parts of units as well as whole units. The decimal point is used to separate the units from the parts of a unit.

Decimal place: The digits used for parts of a unit, such as tenths and hundredths. For example, if a number is given to "2 decimal places," it means that there are digits in the tenths and hundredths columns.

Decimal point: A dot written after the units when a number contains parts of a unit as well as whole numbers.

Denominator: The number written on the bottom of a fraction.

Digit: The numerals 1, 2, 3, 4, 5, 6, 7, 8, 9, or 0. Several may be used to stand for a larger number. They are called digits to make it clear that they are only part of a complete number. So we might say, "The second digit is 4," meaning the second numeral from the left. Or we might say, "That is a two-digit number," meaning that it has two numerals in it, tens and units.

Dividend: The number you wish to divide into.

Divisor: The number you divide with.

Exchanging: In subtracting this is the method of taking 1 from the column to the left to use it as 10 at the top of your working column, and adding 1 at the bottom of the left column. *x*

Flat: A large square representing 100. It can also be made up of ten "longs" put side by side.

Long: A long shape representing 10.

Numerator: The number written on the top of a fraction.

Pi: The number of times bigger the circumference of a circle is than the diameter. It is given a special name because it cannot be written down precisely as a fraction or as a decimal. It is approximately $^{22}/_7$ or 3.14159265….

Quotient: The answer when you divide a dividend by a divisor.

Recurring decimal: A decimal that shows new digits however many decimal places are used. There is always a repeating pattern, so although the digits go on forever, we know what they are.

Regrouping: In subtracting this is the method of moving 1 from the top of the column to the left to use it as 10 at the top of your working column. *See* Exchanging.

Rounding: Making a number simpler.

Significant figures: The numbers (reading from the left) that you need for your purpose. This is a way of describing how precise the number is. It is not affected by the position of the decimal point, which has more to do with the units being used.

Unit: 1 of something. A small square shape representing 1.

Units: A word used with measurement. For example, metric units.

Set index

USING THE SET INDEX

The 13 volumes in the *Math Matters!* set are:

Volume number	Title
1:	**Numbers**
2:	**Adding**
3:	**Subtracting**
4:	**Multiplying**
5:	**Dividing**
6:	**Decimals**
7:	**Fractions**
8:	**Shape**
9:	**Size**
10:	**Tables and Charts**
11:	**Grids and Graphs**
12:	**Chance and Average**
13:	**Mental Arithmetic**

An example entry:

Index entries are listed alphabetically.

numerator **6:** 32, 33; **7:** 7, 36

The volume number is shown in bold for each entry. In this case the index entry for "numerator" is found in two titles: **Decimals** and **Fractions**.
The page references in each volume are shown in regular type. In this case pages 32 and 33 of the tile **Decimals** and pages 7 and 36 of the title **Fractions**.

A

abacus **1:** 6
acute angle **8:** 9, 18
adding **2:** 4–5, 6–7, 8–9; **13:** 20–23, 34, 35, 36, 39
    decimals **2:** 36–37; **6:** 14–17
    fractions **2:** 40–41; **7:** 10–11, 16, 17, 22, 23, 27, 28, 29
    improper fractions **7:** 28
    large numbers **2:** 35
    minus numbers **2:** 38–39
    mixed fractions **7:** 16–17
    mixed numbers **7:** 29
    similar fractions **7:** 10–11
    single-digit numbers **2:** 6–25
    three-digit numbers **2:** 32–33
    two-digit numbers **2:** 28–29
    unlike fractions **7:** 22–23
    using columns **2:** 16–17
    using patterns **2:** 12–13
    using rulers **2:** 10–11
    using shapes **2:** 26–27
adding and subtracting **3:** 8
adding facts **2:** 14–15, 20–23; **3:** 16
adding on **13:** 26–27, 30–31
adding square **2:** 20–21, 24–25
angles **8:** 6–11, 44; **9:** 4, 34–41
    triangles **9:** 38, 39, 40, 41
apex **8:** 41
Arabic numerals **1:** 9
arc **8:** 38; **9:** 35
area **9:** 4, 18–29
    rectangles **9:** 20–21, 26, 27, 28, 29
    squares **9:** 18–19, 24–25
    triangles **9:** 22–23, 24, 25, 26, 27
arrowheads **8:** 31, 33
average **12:** 22–39
    mean **12:** 26–27, 29, 33
    median **12:** 24–25, 27, 28 34–35, 36–37
    mode **12:** 22–23, 27, 28, 34–37
axes **10:** 16, 18, 23; **11:** 16, 17

B

Babylonian number systems **1:** 12, 14
bar charts **10:** 16–17, 18, 21
base **9:** 22
big numbers **1:** 26–27
boundary **8:** 38; **9:** 6, 7

C

calculator check
    decimals **6:** 36
    factors, multiples, and products **4:** 13
    percentages **7:** 37, 41
    square roots **4:** 17
    Turn-Around Rule **4:** 11
capacity **9:** 5, 31
cards **12:** 10, 12, 13
carrying **2:** 23, 28, 29, 30, 31, 33, 35; **5:** 22, 23
categories **10:** 9, 16, 17, 18, 19
chance **12:** 6–21
    decimal numbers **12:** 14–15
    dice **12:** 5, 13, 16–17
    equal chance **12:** 10, 11, 13
    even **12:** 8–9
    fractions **12:** 14–15
    meaning of **12:** 6–7
    percentages **12:** 14–15
    ratios **12:** 14–15, 42–43
charts **10:** 5, 12, 13, 16–43
Chinese numerals **1:** 8
circles **8:** 38, 39
circles and triangles **9:** 35
circular protractor **10:** 43
circumference **8:** 38; **9:** 12, 13, 14, 15
clocks **1:** 13, 15
column charts **10:** 17, 18–19, 20, 21, 22, 23, 38
comparing decimals **6:** 42–43
computers **1:** 13
cones **8:** 40, 42, 43
conversion graphs **11:** 28–37
    Celsius to Fahrenheit **11:** 36–37
    centimeters to inches **11:** 32–33
    Fahrenheit to Celsius **11:** 36–37
    gallons to liters **11:** 28–29
    inches to centimeters **11:** 32–33
    kilograms to pounds **11:** 34–35
    kilometers to miles **11:** 30–31
    liters to gallons **11:** 28–29
    miles to kilometers **11:** 30–31
    pounds to kilograms **11:** 34–35
coordinates **1:** 37; **11:** 14, 16, 18, 19, 20
counting **1:** 7, 12, 22; **2:** 6–7; **3:** 6–7, 10–11
counting numbers **1:** 38

counting systems **1:** 12–13, 22–23
cubes **8:** 40, 41
cubic unit **9:** 31
cuboid **9:** 31
cuneiform writing **1:** 7
cylinders **8:** 40, 42, 43

D

data **10:** 5, 6–7, 9
data table **10:** 8–9
decimal currencies **6:** 10–11
decimal number **6:** 4, 6–7, 8–9
decimal place **6:** 22, 23, 25, 26, 27
decimal point **6:** 6–7, 8–9, 28, 29, 41
decimals **6:** 4, 5, 6–7, 8–9; **13:** 19
    dividing **5:** 26–27
decimal system **6:** 4, 10
degrees **1:** 12, 13, 14; **9:** 34
denominator **6:** 32–33; **7:** 7, 36
designs **8:** 40, 41, 42
diagonal **8:** 30, 31
diameter **8:** 38; **9:** 12, 13, 14, 16, 17
digit **1:** 16; **6:** 31
discount **7:** 41
disk **8:** 42, 43
distance charts **2:** 34–35
dividing **5:** 4–5, 6–7, 8–9, 10–11
    decimals **5:** 26–27; **6:** 30–31, 32, 33, 40–41
    fractions **5:** 30, 31, 34–35
dividing line **5:** 34–35: **7:** 7
division equations **5:** 42–43
division fact **5:** 16

E

easy pairs **13:** 12–13, 14, 15
Egyptian numerals **1:** 8
enlarging shapes **9:** 42–43
equals **1:** 24–25; **2:** 42–43
equations **2:** 42–43; **3:** 8, 9, 42–43; **4:** 8, 9, 30, 31, 42–43
equilateral triangle **7:** 9; **8:** 12, 13, 14, 18, 19, 21, 23, 41; **9:** 34
equivalent fractions **5:** 36–37; **7:** 16–21
even numbers **1:** 38; **3:** 14–15, 16, 17
exchanging method of subtracting **3:** 24–25, 30, 31, 32, 33, 35; **6:** 18–19; **13:** 28

F

fact family **3:** 17
factors **4:** 12–13
flats **1:** 18, 19; **6:** 8, 9
flip symmetry **8:** 22, 23, 24, 25, 26, 27
formula **9:** 10, 11

fractions **7:** 4–5, 6–7
    adding **7:** 10–11, 16, 17, 22, 23, 27, 28, 29
    bigger than one — *see* improper fractions
    comparing **7:** 19
    conversion from decimals **6:** 32–33
    conversion to decimals **6:** 38–39
    multiplying **7:** 12–13
    subtracting **7:** 24–25, 31
    writing **7:** 7
fractions and division **5:** 30, 31, 34–35

G

gate check **10:** 12, 13
gear ratio **7:** 33
geometry symbols **8:** 44
glossary **1–13:** 45
graph **11:** 4, 16–43
Greek numerals **1:** 9
grids **11:** 8, 9, 10, 11
grouping data **10:** 26, 27

H

halves **7:** 6
halving and adding **13:** 36, 39
halving and doubling **13:** 37
height **9:** 22, 30
hexagon **8:** 12, 13, 43
Hindu numerals **1:** 9

I

improper fractions **7:** 26–27, 28, 29, 30
inside angle **8:** 6, 15, 30
isosceles triangle **8:** 18, 19, 32; **9:** 41

K

kites **8:** 31, 33

L

latitude **11:** 8, 9
length **9:** 4, 6, 8, 12, 16–17, 18, 20, 22, 30
less than **1:** 24–25
line charts **10:** 38–39
line equations **11:** 24, 25, 26, 27
line graphs **1:** 36–37; **10:** 36–37; **11:** 23–43
line of symmetry **8:** 22
long division **5:** 18–19, 24–25, 27
longitude **1:** 14, 15; **11:** 8, 9
long multiplication **4:** 32–39, 41
longs **1:** 18, 19; **5:** 10–11; **6:** 8, 9

M

many-fold symmetry **8:** 24–25
maps **11:** 6–13
mental arithmetic **13:** 4–5, 6, 8
mental map **11:** 6–7
minus **3:** 8, 9, 37
minus coordinates **11:** 20
minus numbers **1:** 30–31; **3:** 37, 38, 39
mixed numbers **7:** 26, 27, 28–29
more than **1:** 24–25
multiples **1:** 35, 38; **4:** 12–13, 14
multiplication and division **5:** 16, 17
multiplication facts **4:** 18, 19, 22; **5:** 9, 16, 17
multiplication square **4:** 18–21, 22; **13:** 32, 33
multiplication tables **4:** 18, 19, 22–23; **13:** 32, 33
multiplying **4:** 4–5, 6; **13:** 20, 21, 32–33, 34, 35, 40, 41
    decimal numbers **4:** 40–41; **6:** 22–29
    fractions **7:** 12–13
    using grids **4:** 8, 9, 10, 11, 27, 32–33, 36–37
    using parentheses **4:** 30–31
    using pictures **4:** 7, 8, 9, 10, 11

N

near doubles **13:** 38–39
nets **8:** 40 — *see* designs
number line **2:** 10
number patterns **1:** 38–43
number squares **1:** 42–43
number triangles **1:** 40–41, 43
numbered categories **10:** 24, 25
numbers **1:** 4–5
    as decimals **1:** 32–33
    as fractions **1:** 32–33
    as graphs **1:** 36–37
    as shapes **1:** 18–19
    as symbols — *see* numerals
    origins **1:** 6–7
numerals **1:** 8–11, 17
numerator **6:** 32, 33; **7:** 7, 36

O

obtuse angle **8:** 9, 18
octagon **8:** 12, 13
odd numbers **1:** 38; **13:** 14, 15, 16, 17
odds **12:** 42–43
options **12:** 13
ordered numbers **1:** 22–23; **11:** 18
outside angle **8:** 6, 30
ovals **8:** 38, 39

P

parallelograms **8:** 15, 31, 34–35
parentheses **4:** 30–31
pentagon **8:** 12, 13, 43
per, a word for divide **5:** 38–39
percent **7:** 36–43; **13:** 36, 37
    conversion to fractions **7:** 38–39
percentage — *see* percent
percent less **7:** 42–43
percent more **7:** 40–41
perimeter **9:** 6–15
    circles **9:** 12–15
    pentagon **9:** 8
    rectangles **9:** 8, 10–11
    squares **9:** 10–11
perpendicular lines **8:** 9, 16, 17
pi **1:** 15; **6:** 39; **9:** 14, 15
pictograms **10:** 14, 15, 16
pie-chart measurer **10:** 41
pie charts **10:** 40–43
place value **1:** 2, 16–17, 18, 19; **2:** 2;
    3: 2; **4:** 2; **5:** 2; **6:** 2; **7:** 2; **9:** 2;
    10: 2; **13:** 2
plus numbers **3:** 38, 39
polyhedron **8:** 41
powers **1:** 27
prime factors **4:** 14, 15
prime numbers **1:** 34, 35, 38; **4:** 14–15
products **4:** 12–13
proportion **7:** 34–35
protractor **9:** 35
pyramids **8:** 41

Q

quadrilaterals **8:** 13, 30–31
quarters **7:** 6, 8–9, 10–11, 12

R

radius **8:** 18, 19, 38; **9:** 13
rainfall charts **10:** 34–35
range **12:** 30–33, 34, 36–37
ratios **5:** 40–41; **7:** 32–33, 35
ray **8:** 9
rectangles **8:** 25, 31, 36–37
recurring decimals **6:** 33, 34–35, 39
reflection **8:** 22, 23
regrouping **13:** 29
regrouping method of subtracting
    3: 26–27, 28, 29; **6:** 20–21
regular shapes **8:** 12–13
remainder **5:** 22, 23, 24, 25, 28–31, 39
    as a decimal **5:** 39
    as a fraction **5:** 30–31
rhombus **8:** 31, 35

right angle **8:** 8, 9, 18, 44; **9:** 34
right-angled triangles **8:** 16–17, 18, 21
rods **8:** 40, 42, 43
Roman numerals **1:** 10–11
rounding **1:** 28–29; **7:** 41
    decimals **6:** 28, 29, 36–37
    down **1:** 28–29
    up **1:** 28–29

S

samples **12:** 40–41
scale **10:** 20–21, 22, 23, 29, 34
scales **11:** 14, 16
sectors **8:** 39
set square **9:** 34, 38, 39
shape **8:** 4–5
sharing **5:** 8–9
short division **5:** 12–15, 22, 26
short multiplication **4:** 24-27
Sieve of Eratosthenes **4:** 15
significant figures **6:** 42, 43
similar fractions **7:** 10–11
size **9:** 4–5
solid shapes **8:** 40–43; **9:** 30–33
sorting category **10:** 16, 18
spheres **8:** 40, 43
splitting-up numbers **13:** 8–9
Splitting-Up Rule **4:** 30–31
spread **10:** 32, 33; **12:** 30–31, 33, 37,
    38–39
square numbers **4:** 16–17, 20
square roots **1:** 42, 43; **4:** 16–17
squares **8:** 12, 13, 15, 24, 31, 37
straight angle **8:** 9, 10, 11; **9:** 38
subtracting **3:** 4–5; **13:** 24–31, 34, 35
    across zero **3:** 36–39
    decimals **3:** 32–33; **6:** 18–21
    fractions **3:** 40–41; **7:** 24–25, 31
    improper fractions **7:** 30
    large numbers **3:** 28–29
    minus numbers **3:** 37, 38, 39
    mixed numbers **7:** 30–31
    numbers with zeros **3:** 30–31
    similar fractions **3:** 40–41
    single-digit numbers **3:** 20–21, 22
    two-digit numbers **3:** 22–23
    using columns **3:** 20–23, 28–33
    using number lines **3:** 8–9, 12–13,
        36–37
    using patterns **3:** 10, 14–17
    using rulers **3:** 8–9, 12–13
    using shapes **3:** 18–24
subtracting and dividing **5:** 6–7
subtracting facts **3:** 14–17

Sumerian numbers **1:** 7
symbols **1–13:** 44
symmetry **8:** 22–27

T

tables **10:** 5, 8–9, 10–11, 12–13
tally charts **10:** 12, 13, 14, 15, 16, 18
tallying **10:** 12–13
tessellating shapes **8:** 28–29
tetrahedron **8:** 41
three-dimensional (3D) shapes **8:** 4, 40,
    41, 43
time charts **10:** 28–31
times tables **4:** 22–23
total **4:** 13
trapeziums **8:** 31, 32–33
triangles **8:** 14–19, 22–23, 28, 29,
    32, 39
Turn-Around Rule **2:** 18–19, 25;
    4: 10-11, 18, 19, 22, 35;
    13: 10, 11
turning symmetry **8:** 23, 24–25, 26, 27
two-dimensional (2D) shapes **8:** 4,
    12–39

U

unit **6:** 8, 9; **7:** 12
units **1:** 18, 19
    in division **5:** 10–11
unit squares **9:** 18–19
unordered numbers **1:** 22–23
using pictures **13:** 6–7

V

vertex **8:** 7, 41
volumes **9:** 4, 5, 30–33
    cuboid **9:** 30–31
    cylinder **9:** 32
    pyramid **9:** 33
    rod **9:** 32

W

whole number **1:** 17, 35
whole numbers **6:** 5, 6
width **9:** 11, 18, 20, 22, 30

X

x-axis **11:** 16, 20

Y

y-axis **11:** 16, 20

Z

zero **1:** 20–21, 26, 27